No women allowed on floodplain during ceremony

Magwanydjuwa Flood Plain

Iridiyu – Camp site when f...

Restricted Area

Mabil

Wob...

Do not touch

No entry without permission

Oenpelli

Garrkany Camp Site

Iliwara

Fishing Place

East

Badpanawarr Jabiru nest

ARNHEM

KADU

Forest

NATIONAL

PARK

LAND

Paperbark

Nadab – floodplain closeup to Ubirr

Alligator

Monsoon

Forest

River

Ubirr

Galleries

Big Bill Neidjie
of the Gagudju people.
'Kakadu' is derived from
Gagudju.

National Library of Australia
Cataloguing-in-Publication entry
Neidjie, Bill, 1913-
Davis, Stephen, 1951-
Fox, Allan, 1931-
Kakadu Man . . . Bill Neidjie.

ISBN 0 9589458 0 2
1. Aboriginal life — Australia.

This book was made possible through financial assistance
from the Department of Aboriginal Affairs, Canberra,
Australia.

Australia's KAKADU MAN
BILL NEIDJIE

Big Bill Neidjie   Stephen Davis   Allan Fox

Resource Managers
Darwin

Foreword

IN 1985, much of white Australia is coming to terms with many of the concepts of black Australia. These concepts have been more than 40,000 years in the making. 40,000 years in which Australia's indigenous people learned to live in harmony with an environment of great variety where climatic factors varied enormously and where a stark and at times terrifying beauty gave birth to the legend of the dreamtime.

Australia has always been a hard and difficult land, and the lessons of survival learnt by Aboriginal inhabitants can still be of great relevance to many parts of Australia today.

The Bunitj land of Bill Neidjie is part of Aboriginal Australia and the words of Bill Neidjie in this book can give us all a valuable and precious insight into that world.

In all the years that I have known him, Bill Neidjie's concern has been to care for his land, to preserve his traditions and his dreaming, and to see that the law and the dreaming are passed on to his grandchildren. It was that concern which some time ago led Bill Neidjie to make the important decision to entrust his stories and much of his dreaming to a young anthropologist, Stephen Davis, who by recording it in written form would ensure that it was never lost (to his grandchildren and to the Bunitj people).

Bill Neidjie and the Bunitj people have leased to the Commonwealth of Australia all of their land so that it now forms part of the Kakadu National Park. In doing so, the wish of the Bunitj people was that the Commonwealth could jointly care for their land, cherish it, and preserve it as part of a permanent natural area to be enjoyed by all Australians in the time ahead.

In all the arguments for and against Aboriginal Land Rights, it has seldom been brought to public attention that no single group of Australian people have acted with the generosity of spirit, that the Aboriginal people in the East Alligator River region have shown in their preparedness to lease to the Commonwealth all of their land in order that it can become part of one large wild area. I can think of no other comparable act in recent Australian history, where any other private or commercial group of citizens have been prepared to place any Government body, in a position of acting as a trustee in the national interests, over land for which they hold private title. Much of this land has enormous potential tourist attraction.

Within the Bunitj lands of Bill Neidjie there stands Ubirr (Obiri Rock), a major centre of tourist attraction in the Northern Territory. The rock contains some of the best examples of unique, prehistoric rock art in the world. Paintings which predate the pyramids by 15,000 years form part of the greatest prehistoric rock art collection in the world. This collection is also unique because unlike other prehistoric collections such as those found in Europe, the galleries of the West Arnhem Land region are part of a *continuous and prevailing contemporary Aboriginal culture.*

It is the preservation of this culture and the understanding of this tradition which will enable a broader multi-cultural Australian society to come to terms with its own history.

The words of Bill Neidjie encompassed in this book will add greatly to that understanding. Bill Neidjie makes no apology for his Aboriginality or his commitment to Aboriginal law and custom...he is Aboriginal and proud of it.

It is part of his being. It is part of the totality of the man.

As the commercialism of an aggressive, materialistic and dominant white society increasingly impinges upon the Gagudju people, it is inevitable that there will be from time to time, a clash of culture and a clash of values.

It is one of the presumptions that has characterised white occupation of Australia that in almost every instance we regard *our* values as being those which must transcend in any conflict situation.

It has been bluntly if not brutally put by Mr. Justice Fox in his report: "They (Aboriginals) are a community whose lives have been, and are still being, disrupted by the intrusions of an alien people. They feel the pressures of the white man's activities in relations to their land. In the face of mining exploration, and the threat of much further development, they feel helpless and lost. Their culture and their traditional social organisation do not enable them to cope with the many problems and questions to which this development gives rise. Their custom is to arrive at important decisions after long deliberation among themselves, sometimes over a period of months or even years. In relations to matters outside tribal tradition, they have not delegated authority to make decisions to any one or more persons...their concerns and values are different from those held by the white man." I am hopeful that in time, the values of a dominant white community will be sufficiently flexible to encompass within it some of the valuable insights that Aboriginal people learnt in their 50,000 years occupation of its land. If that is possible, then Australia will not only be a more compassionate and caring society, it will be a society in harmony with itself and its environment.

The words of Bill Neidjie can thus provide us with an insight, and possibly an understanding, of a tradition and a culture far older than anything that has thus far prevailed in Europe, and hopefully give all a new insight and perception of our own land, and our need to care for it and preserve it.

The Honourable Clyde Holding MP
Minister for Aboriginal Affairs
Canberra 1984

Australian dreaming

THE OCCUPATION OF AUSTRALIA by humans probably began as long ago as 50,000 years when, during a period of low sea level, a small group of coastal people made a remarkable ocean voyage across the final gap separating this land from the Indonesian lowlands. No one will ever know what drove these people on. It is unlikely that population pressure directly was the cause now that the vast inter-island Sunda plains had been exposed by the retreating sea of an ice age. Was it the seasonal drift of smoke from the greatly increased area of woodlands from over the south-eastern horizon which lured them on...or did the steady north-west monsoon which, along with bamboo and other flotsam including people on flimsy rafts, simply drive them here like it drove the later Maccassans and Vietnamese?

Whatever reason or by whatever agency they came, these were people of the coasts, people who lived by the sea and with the sea. Once they had conquered the problem of flotation, their arrival was inevitable. They arrived not as an invading force and not as purposeful colonists, but as "lost" people saved when they beached on the long low shores of north-western Australia. Whatever their mode of arrival, they came long, long ago... perhaps two thousand generations before even the pyramids where built.

Eight generations ago, Cook's belated "discoveries" set in motion the forces which have all but destroyed this Aboriginal culture rooted in 50,000 years of experience in the Australian environment. A vision of the richness and depth of that experience comes through in Big Bill Neidjie's wisdom. But we get ahead of our story...

Much of Bill's land is on the productive lowland – Magela Ck.

The two ancestors came ashore at Malay Bay – Arnhem coast.

They came on wind and tide and "created" a new land...

Like the turtles they came ashore, and on the featureless land they left their tracks – Flatback Turtle, Field Is.

It is most likely that the ancestor Aboriginals arrived at a time when a glacial period was in full swing. The sea level had dropped some 100 metres. The last time the levels were as low as that was from 15,000 to 20,000 years BP, but at that time there were people grinding their tools near the caverns by the East Alligator (a world first in technology) and Aboriginals by then had been camping by Lake Mungo for at least 10,000–15,000 years. The low level previous to the last, was between 55 and 50,000 years BP. That is a likely arrival period.

Even with these low sea levels the trip to Australia required a substantial voyage of up to ninety kilometres, making the ancestors perhaps the first mariners, landing on a combined North Australian New Guinean coast which was then seawards 300–500 kilometres north west of the present coast.

The beach and what lay ahead was a vast unknown plain in the minds of these very early navigators. The oceanic gap separated the Australian realm from the Asian...tigers and leopards gave way to thylacines and marsupial lion...buffalo, rhinoceros and pigs to diprotodons, kangaroos, and wallabies... monkeys to koalas, possums and phalangers. Two worlds had drifted close enough for humans to enter and to be nonplussed by the old Australians. Some northerners, the rodents for instance had made it earlier while some other animals were common to both worlds, the crocodiles and turtles.

But like Neil Armstrong or Columbus, those first settlers must have found Australia/New Guinea as a new and mysterious place.

The first people were navigators with a tradition of food, shelter and understandings which where coastal. As the ancestors moved about the land, they saw, remembered and explained the features. So far as humans were concered they created by their discoveries, a "new" landscape, just as Columbus had "created" the Americas for Spaniards.

As a child builds up a perception of place through accumulated experience so these early generations assembled a richer and richer accumulation of perceptions of landscape, of habitat. Place was associated with natural phenomena particularly powerful elements such as lightning, floods, fire and volcanoes. To give authority and coherence to the perceptions so that they could be effectively accumulated and passed on from generation to generation, creation heroes became tied into and linked the growing net of perceptions. The environment and humans were becoming parts of the same processes of the living world.

Over the generations, traditions of the people developed an incredible complexity which became woven into the structure of society, into the relationships between people, between people and their habitat and between ages of experience. Accumulated experience became so great that even the oldest individual could not retain it all. Without a written language this wisdom of the people remained in many living minds...but the minds were living in a landscape every part of which was a "permanent" reminder of perception and explanation. The landscape therefore is critical in maintaining the Aboriginals' physical, mental and spiritual life. These latter sites are referred to as "sacred sites", but does the word sacred have the depth of meaning to describe the values involved?

So, through 50,000 or more years, the environment which sustained life and culture became bound intimately with every aspect of human life...Aboriginal and environment were one and the same. Ownership of land in the European sense did not exist. Aboriginals were part of the living systems because through their mythology they understood that their ancestors created the landscape and the life on it including themselves, with each part playing a role in the maintenance of the whole dynamic world.

The most important role that an individual human could play in this system was that of custodian of the common environment.

First chairman of the Northern Land Council, Silas Roberts, put it this way:

> "Aboriginals have a special connection with everything that is natural. Aboriginals see themselves as part of nature. We see all things natural as part of us. All the things on Earth we see as part human. This is told through the idea of dreaming. By dreaming we mean the belief that long ago, these creatures started human society.
>
> These creatures, these great creatures are just as much alive today as they were in the beginning. They are everlasting and will never die. They are always part of the land and nature as we are. Our connection to all things natural is spiritual."

Stephen Davis while teaching at Millingimbi, Arnhem Land made many offshore fishing trips with local Aboriginal people. He soon became aware that his hosts avoided some areas of water and consistently turned back when the boat drifted across seemingly imaginary lines. When asked for an explanation the people shrugged and said that that place was someone else's place. Triangulating features along the coast from the boat Davis found that the places of turnaround were indeed consistent. Davis has now made many miles of soundings along the north coast and around Bathurst and Melville Islands. In each instance he has found that the "imaginery" lines follow undersea ridges and valley bottoms. Accurately bound into traditional behaviour is knowledge of ice-age geography, a landscape that dissappeared thousands of years before the birth of Christ. Some places under 30 meters of water are still maintained as sacred sites. To coastal people, land and water were one and the same...the sea has had them in retreat but tradition has it that one day they will return to their submerged land.

With rising sea levels following melting of the ice, the meandering lower reaches of the Alligator Rivers became tidal estuaries, mud building up along the banks cut off side

backswamps and mudflats. Sands were swept by wave, current and tide into bars and spits building beach ridges between points, cutting off and forming lagoon systems. Each bar, ridge and lagoon formed new zones for life, the mangroves moved in, some 21 species, along with the animal components of these rich nurseries of marine life.

East Alligator River, created by ancestors.

Geography and seasonality ruled the Aboriginal lives through their effect on access and food supply...not so much controlling the shortage of food but the maintenance of variety. Seasonal changes ushered in new foods. The Aboriginal seasonal calendar emphasises this point even in the very simple form presented. To indicate the complex understandings which have developed I quote from the Arnhem Land Environ Series published by the Millingimbi Literature Production Centre...Book 4, "Rrarranhdharr".

"We know that Dharratharramirri (season) is coming to an end when balgurr (*Brachychiton paradoxis*) starts to lose its leaves. At the same time the pandanus (Gunga: *Pandanus yirrkalensis*) starts to fruit and Dhimurru (East-South-East) wind blows. The really cold mornings and mists are nearly gone. Sharks are giving birth to their young. They are called burrugu and so we call this season Burrugumirri. This is a very short season which only lasts for a few weeks. Stingrays are also called burrugu at this time. If munydjutj (*Buchanania obovata*) is flowering, then we are really sure that they are fat..."

How fascinating it is to see the flowering of a plant as an indicator of stingrays being fat!...and how much experience and memory was needed to distil that relationship.

After doing his work Indjuwanydjuwa settled into the mud of Red Lily billabong.

This deeply integrated view of the human environment rests on the fact that the Aboriginal landscape has become fully personalised. But how is such a store of tradition passed on particularly without a written language?

It happens primarily because life and learning are synonymous. Even a cursory look at the Bunitj year will illustrate the point. Tradition is continuously demonstrated and practised as a staged learning process culminating at its richest point at the moment of death. Transmission is by way of myth, stories, field experiences, play, song cycles, dances, pattern and design of artefacts and the ritual of ceremonies.

In the beginning the Bunitj land was a blank plain. An ancestral being, Indjuwanydjuwa (In-joo-won-i-joowa) travelled this landscape in his daily activities, hunting, gathering food, performing rituals, within the context of giving form to the landscape. He lived in a rock shelter on the wall of which was his picture...at his own volition following his acts of creation he turned himself into a great stone standing in a billabong surrounded by a "sea" of pink lotus. A chain of sites of varying importance define the route of his travels. The maintenance of these, their stories, rituals and songs is the responsibility of the senior man of the clan. This maintenance includes the protection of visitors who might blunder onto dangerous sites. Some of the ancestors' movements took them into and across lands occupied by adjoining clans...the stories and ceremonies related to these movements are shared and jointly enacted.

A number of ancestral beings may have been involved in the

creation of the landscape and its biota including the humans. Some of these beings were female. One here was involved in the birth of the Bunitj language group. The senior resident woman is responsible for the female sites and the stories. The form of the area and its biota then is the map of the activities of the ancestors. Bill Neidjie puts it in this way:

"Rock stays
Earth stays
I die and put may bones in cave or earth
Soon my bones become earth...
All the same
My spirit has gone back to my country...
My mother."

"Our story is in the land...
It is written in those sacred places."

The art of living...

The coastal lowlands of the East Alligator River has been exposed by the retreating sandstone Arnhem Land Plateau. At lower sea levels the rivers cut broad valleys in the ancient basement rocks. In places, isolated outliers of sandstone rise like islands from the lowland ridges. Subsequently the broad valleys filled with mud and became swampy plains. During wet seasons these plains became a vast wetland. Probably half of the Bunitj land goes under water.

Four distinct food producing zones are used at varying times according to the seasons...black soil floodplain, stone country of the outliers and plateau, monsoon forest (jungle) and eucalypt woodland/forest. Some of the major food items are:

Black Soil	Stone Country	Monsoon Forest	Eucalypt
Barramundi	Rock Wallabies	Yams	Kangaroos
File Snakes	Wallaroos	Possums	Wallabies
Crocodiles	Anteaters	Bush Apples	Frill-neck lizards
Turtles	Goannas	Flying Foxes	Blue-tongue
Water Lilies	Pythons	Lizards	lizards
Bustards	Figs		Honey
Geese			Plums
Ducks			Emus

Before the coming of the whites probably 40–60 people lived on this area augmented from time to time by visits from adjoining clans. Some camps as at Ubirr (Obiri) were regularly used by eight clans but always after permission had been sought from the traditional owner.

Movement was initiated by changes in food supply, comfort, ceremonies and the seasons. A man walking alone would cover 15–30 kms a day while a family with children would travel 8–10 kms between camps. Some traditional walks which linked people into a sequence of ceremonial activity and renewal of relationships with country were of considerable magnitude...the Badmardi Clan of Kakadu had a recorded two month marathon of some 600 kms.

One could write much more about the depth of knowledge these people have of the natural community to which they and we belong, but it should be quite apparent now that they are continuously learning the processes of living and that the landscape itself is not only teacher but text book as well. In every physical and metaphysical way they are inextricably bound into the Australian systems. These ecosystems themselves were also to varying degrees artifacts of the relationship...fire being the obvious tool in this process. I can find no adequate word in English to describe the personalisation of the landscape by Aboriginals. It is little wonder then that when Europeans arrived they had no capacity to understand what they described at best as simple people. They looked not for a harmonious relationship but for evidence of ownership, of manipulation, of control, not a relationship more akin to membership...many still do.

The words of Big Bill Neidjie are a first attempt by an old Aboriginal to pass on to all people some of the wisdom accumulated from the experience of 2000 or more generations. I have known Bill 8 years and this has been his greatest concern, that his own children and others will "hang onto" this knowledge, this wisdom. If we later Australians are only wise enough to listen, it maybe that we will still have enough time to cure some of the environmental calamities initiated by our clumsy steward-ship...Bill is on about *attitudes and values*...the future rests on ours.

Allan Fox

BUNITJ YEAR OF
CHANGING SEASONS

Gunumeleng (October to December) is the pre-
monsoon season of hot weather which becomes more
and more humid. Winds are mixed up, swinging right
around the compass with storm clouds building and
rumbling in the afternoons. Billabongs and waterholes
become dry and cracked. Magpie Geese crowd around
and Long-necked Turtles shelter underground. Drought
is broken by thunderstorms and life once again returns.
New vegetation fattens insects and these, the frogs,
reptiles, birds and mammals, including Bunitj people.
It is time to move camp from the floodplain.

Igalkal.
Magpie Geese.
Varanus glebapalma.

16

Gudjewg (January to March) is the monsoon season, the 'wet'. Already the spring tides are covering the lowlands, first flooding since the last 'wet' and by January's end the rains have filled the wetlands. There is heavy growth throughout the whole bush. Every day the north-west wind brings in the cloud from the sea – there is no thunder just heavy rain and strong winds. Lorikeets swarm over the flowering eucalypts after nectar, Magpie Geese are nesting in the sedgeland and barramundi feed into the grasses and are easily speared. But there are many fish and the mangrove worms are deliciously fat. If there is one flowering season, Gudjewg is it.

Twin Falls.
Gould's Goanna, flooded out.
Swamp Bloodwood.

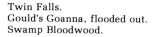

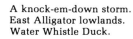

A knock-em-down storm.
East Alligator lowlands.
Water Whistle Duck.

Bang-Gereng (April). The light east wind signals the time of food abundance. Most plants are fruiting and many animals are caring for their young. There is still much water on the lowlands and all the creeks are running clear water from the sandstone. Towards the end of the season the winds swing to the south-east and on the change, violent storms flatten the tall, fragile native sorghum, giving this season its other name – 'of the knock-em-down storms.'

Yegge (May-June). The nights are cool and frequently hazy and misty early in the morning. Wind blows constantly from the south-east drying out the grass. Fires are lit near the campsites and places which will grow green feed over the next few months. Masses of insects move before the fire and are preyed upon by Black Kites and the last of the White-breasted Woodswallows for the year. Many insectivorous and seed-eating birds move south as the season dries. Snakes and flying foxes are a favoured food during Yegge.

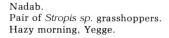

Nadab.
Pair of *Stropis sp.* grasshoppers.
Hazy morning, Yegge.

Wurrgeng (June-July) is the cold weather season when night temperatures may drop as low as 12°c. Dew forms on the grass in June and much burning commences each day to be dampened by dew at night. Food from the estuaries is important in this season – mud crabs and fiddler crabs are taken. Barramundi and mullet move into quiet waters when the south-east wind blows stronger. When the *Pandanus* fruit start to change from green to orange then Wurrgeng is nearly finished. The *Grevillea pteridiifolia* are heavy with flowers and honey.

'Cleaning' the country.
Brindled Bandicoots are disturbed by the grass fires.
Nadab plain dries off.

Gurrung (August-September). The warm south-east wind ripens the Pandanus fruit and the hot-dry season begins. As soon as the Stringybark flowers, snakes lay their eggs and honey is in abundance. Dew and mist is gone – the bush is dry and smoky, smelling continually of scorched eucalypts. Rays and sharks are fat and the turtles will be laying eggs on the sandy beach of Field Is. Gould's Goannas rob the nests. Emus are fat and are hunted along with Brolga, Magpie Geese, the bandicoot and wallaby. The first white-Breasted Wood-swallows arrive as the thunderheads begin to build and the season changes to Gunumeleng.

Birds collect on the shrinking waters of Nadab.
Thunderheads.
Late fires are hot fires.

Bill Neidjie
of the Gagudju

ARCHAEOLOGICAL WORK in the East Alligator River area evidences a continuous occupation of the region by Aboriginal people for the last 25,000 years. Such work also confirms that pigments for painting were prepared at least 18,000 years ago.

During the glacial period of 20,000 years ago when the coast was a further 250 kilometres north and the flood plains perhaps 100 metres above the sea level, the Aboriginal people were fresh water river people, occupying the Alligator Rivers areas. With the melting of the glaciers the sea level rose and the Alligator Rivers environment changed. As the sea approached its present-day level, the area became estuarine and Aboriginal people ranged across a landscape similar to that which we see today. Fish, water lilies and geese were as much a part of the landscape then as they are today.

Aboriginal occupation of the Alligator Rivers area has embraced a time span beyond which most people can conceive. When Moses was leading the exodus from Egypt, Aboriginal occupation of the Alligator Rivers had been continuous for at least 218 centuries. When Christ was embarking on his ministry

'We encamped at this pool, and the natives flocked around us from every direction. Boys of every age, lads, young men and old men too, came, everyone armed with his bundle of goose spears, and his throwing stick' L. Leichhardt – Nov. 1845. Leichhardt Spring.

An interpretation of Leichhardt? Three pools gallery, Kakadu.

in Galilee, Aboriginal people had occupied the Alligator Rivers for almost 230 centuries. The arrival of Captain James Cook in Australia had been preceded then by over 230 centuries of continuous occupation in the Alligator Rivers and across what, in our recorded history, has been identified as the estate of the Gagudju (Kakadu) people and in particular the Bunitj clan estate of Big Bill Neidjie.

The earliest accounts of European contact with the Gagudju come from the explorer Ludwig Leichhardt. In November and December of 1844, Leichhardt and his party travelled through the area noting that the country was well populated.

> The natives were very numerous and employing themselves either in fishing or burning the grass on the plains, or digging for roots. I saw here a noble fig-tree, under the shade of which seemed to have been the camping place of the natives for the last century.
> (Leichhardt 1847 : 493)

The total Aboriginal population of the area at the time of Leichhardt's contact was probably in excess of 2,000 people.

Following European contact, a serious decline in the population took place. In 1922 Paddy Cahill, a well-known buffalo hunter in the region, stated that he would not be able to muster more than 100 Aborigines in the area.

Census figures for the 1960's confirmed fears that there were few local people living. A census return for 1965 lists only two Gagudju people as well as Charlie Whittaker (an elderly Aboriginal friend of Bill Neidjie listed as belonging to the "Gunwinggo"tribe). A 1966 census listed only Bill's close friend Felix Holmes (Iyanuk) of the Limilngan language group and two elderly Gagudju people in the area.

Bill Neidjie is one of the few of the remaining Gagudju.

BIG BILL NEIDJIE

Big Bill Neidjie was born at Alawanydajawany on the East Alligator River in the mid 1920's or earlier. Bill, like is father Nadampala before him, is of the Bunitj clan (gunmugurrkurr), Gagudju language group.

Bill was raised in the East Alligator area. He lived at Ubirr (Obiri Rock) for about one year when his mother Lucy Wirlmaka was about 21 years old. Here he learnt to hunt and to manage the resources of his environment. His father, his grandfather and his uncles instructed Bill in the law.

While Bill was still a child his mother stencilled his hand in ochre on a rock shelter at the site known as Walkarr on the Bunitj clan estate where it remains today.

Bill's mother from the Ulbuk clan of the Amurrak language group, took Bill to live at Cape Don 180 kilometres north of East Alligator when Bill was 12 or 13 years of age. He lived there with his mother's family for 5 or 6 years. "Old Billy Manilugu, we lived with him. He was a buffalo hunter. He knew all the (Aboriginal) law."

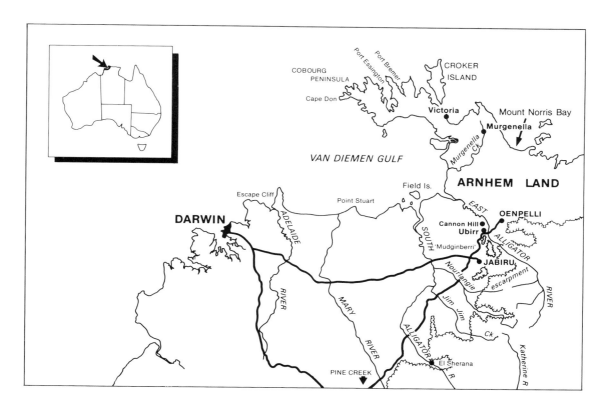

Billy Manilugu was a prominent ceremonial leader throughout the entire region. "He was a big song man". Billy Manilugu taught Bill much of the traditional Aboriginal law. After the second World War, he particularly taught Bill's friend, Iyanuk (Felix Holmes) of the Limilngan clan, many of the songs necessary for the continuance of the Morak ceremonial cycle, of which Bill and Iyanuk are custodians.

Bill returned to East Alligator intermittently until he was about 20 years of age. At that time Bill's mother took up residence at Cape Don on a permanent basis where she stayed until her mother passed away.

As a young man in company with his friend Toby Gangali of the Mirrarr clan, Bill started work with the buffalo hunters at Cannon Hill but did not stay long. "Me and Toby, we used to run away from them buffalo hunters. We were too young".

From about 22 years of age, Bill worked for several years at a timber mill in Mount Norris Bay ("Iwal, that's near Minimini Creek") for Chan Long. Bill then was engaged to cart timber to Darwin in the lugger Maskee. The work continued from Mount Norris Bay until the Mill at Croker Island took over. Bill worked with the Croker mill for a further three years. "There was no mission there then. Soon as war came, mission started for coloured people".

Bill then started work with Leo Hickey on his lugger along the north coast run. On one occasion Leo Hickey, with Bill in

his employ, was engaged to transport 20 to 30 people to the new settlement of Maningrida. But, as Bill relates, the task was not entirely successful. "They did not stay there because after two weeks there were no smokes (cigarettes) left".

During the Second World War, Bill returned to the East Alligator area. He lived at Paw Paw Beach (Murgenella Creek). There an Ubarr ceremony was performed. Participation in an Ubarr ceremony is one of the most important events in a Gagudju man's life. Ruben Cooper, the son, by an Aboriginal woman, of one of the first buffalo hunters, was a senior man overseeing that particular performance of the Ubarr ceremony.

"Ruben Cooper told me to get in that Ubarr. Otherwise it would be too late for me and I would miss it. He said 'In two weeks when you finished that ceremony you come and see me.' Two dozen of us young fellers went in (to be initiated into the ceremony)." Bill and fellow initiates were under the control of senior ceremonial leaders. Severe restrictions are placed on initiates who are isolated during the performance of the Ubarr ceremony including eating and drinking prohibitions. "Those

Bill Neidjie and Iyanuk preparing themselves to repaint part of the Indjuwanydjuwa story on a cavern wall.

26

Loading buffalo products.
These photos taken by Ryko
when Bill was a small boy.

old men never even let us move. They tell us 'see that big well over there? We'll put you in it and you'll be dead if you disobey.' But three men were waiting for us... with spears. 'Where you going?' they say. We were so scared we was shaking all over."

Some time later Ruben Cooper became ill. "There was no medicine so he died. But, half way before he died he said to me 'I don't know if I'll see you again. You look after women and children. You must look after the land.' Then he died."

In recent years Bill has again become a permanent resident on his own land. In 1979 Bill was a claimant in the Alligator Rivers Stage II Land Claim heard before Justice Toohey, the Aboriginal Land Commissioner. The Bunitj people of the Gagudju language group were awarded title to their land as a result of this claim.

The identity of an Aboriginal person, however, is much more than legal title to land. He must fulfil the responsibilities with which his people were charged by ancestral beings in the creative epoch.

For Gagudju Man: Big Bill Neidjie...land is life.

Aboriginal man always been free . . .
just Aboriginal.
But white man . . .
he was slave one time.
Maybe he slave himself,
maybe slave work for him . . .
But no good.

Now white man got learning.
He got university school.
He can read.
But me only read little bit.
White people got computer,
but Aboriginal, me . . .
I just write in cave.

Law written in cave.
That painting is law.

Little Dolly Yanmalu. Bill's sister.

Aboriginal law never change.
Old people tell us . . .
'You gotta keep it'.
It always stay.
Never change.

But learning can be different.
So now I've got to teach my children with book.
They forget how to learn Aboriginal way.
That why I write this book . . .
To bring my children back.

Bringing the Law back.

'I give you this Story'

I give you this story.
This proper, true story.
People can listen.
I'm telling this while you've got time....
time for you to make something,
you know....
history....
book

I was thinking....
no history written for us when white European start here,
only few words written.
Should be more than that.

Should be written way Aborigine was live.
That floodplain....
my father, my mother, my grandfather
all used to hunt there,
use ironwood spear.
No clothes then.

When I was growing up
good mob of people all around then.
Now people bit wicked.
My time never do little bit wrong....
otherwise get spear straight away.
Now.... little bit cheeky mob.
Old time they would all be dead now.
Old people were hard....
I frightened when young.
Only few people now,
but it easy for this mob.

Anyway, got to be made that book.
There's still time.
No man can growl at me for telling this story,
because it will be too late....
I'll be dead.

Introduction

This earth....
I never damage,
I look after.
Fire is nothing,
just clean up.
When you burn,
New grass coming up.
That mean good animal soon....
might be goose, long-neck turtle, goanna, possum.
Burn him off....
new grass coming up,
new life all over.

I don't know about white European way.
We, Aborigine, burn....
Make things grow.
Tree grow,
every night he grow.
Daylight....
he stop.
Just about dark....
he start again.
Just about morning I look.
I say,
'Oh, nice tree this.'

When you sleep,
tree growing like other trees....
they got lots of blood.

Rotten tree....
you got to burn him.
Use him to cook.
He's finished up....
cook or roast in coals.
White European cook in oven....
from university that.
Aborigine didn't know that before.
Now all this coming up with Toyota.

First people come to us,
they started and run our life.... quick.
They bring drink.
First they should ask about fish, cave, dreaming, but....
they rush in.
They make school.... teach.
Now Aborigine losing it,
losing everything.
Nearly all dead my people,
my old people gone.

Those first people was too quick,
wasn't Aborigine fault.
Still Aborigine all around 1929....
1952, 1953 few left but....
1970 to 1979.... gone.
Only me, Robin Gaden and Felix Holmes.

Each man he stay....
stay on his own country.
He can't move his country....
so he stay there,
stay with his language.
Language is different....
like skin.
Skin can be different,
but blood same.
Blood and bone....
all same.
Man can't split himself.

White European can't say
'Oh, that Aborigine no good.'
Might be that Aborigine alright.
Man can't growl at Aborigine,
Aborigine can't growl at white European....
Because both ways.
Might be both good men,
might be both no good....
you never know.

So you should get understand yourself.
No matter Aborigine or white European.
I was keeping this story myself.
It was secret in my mind,
but I see what other people doing,
and I was feeling sad.

Law

Law never change....
always stay same.
Maybe it hard,
but proper one for all people.

Not like white European law....
always changing.
If you don't like it,
you can change.

Aboriginal law never change.
Old people tell us,
'You got to keep it.'
It always stays.

Creek, plain, hill.
That plain can change....
wet season, him mud.
You get lily,
you get fish.
But, he dry up....
that's alright.
Then people can get long-neck turtle.
Same for animal.
People look for food,
animal look for food.
Lizard look,
bird look,
anyone look.
We all same.

Each billabong can be dry....
no fish, turtle, nothing.
He want new water,
then fish and turtle,
make him new one.
New rain coming up,
that rain make everything again....
plenty fish, turtle, lily.

Rain for us....
for anybody.
Rain give us everything new....
yam, fish, everything.

Barramundi good in the wet season...
still good after the wet because of rain.
Big Barramundi from salt water.
He follow fresh water down river,
rain helping him.
He can make eggs.

We must get rain.
Law says we get rain.
He come along wet season and go dry season.
Rain come down and give us new fresh water.
Plants coming up new....
yam, creeper all plants new.
Then we get fruit, honey and things to live.

Tree, he change with rain.
He get new leaf,
he got to come because rain.
Yam he getting big too.

Old people say
'You dig yam?
Well you digging your granny or mother....
through the belly.
You must cover it up,
cover again.
When you get yam you cover over,
then no hole through there.
Yam can grow again.'

'You hang onto this story' they say.
So I hang on.
I tell kids.
When they get yam, leave hole,
I say
'Who leave that hole?
Cover him up.'
They say
'We forget.'
I tell them
'You leaving hole....
you killing yam.
You killing yourself.
You hang onto your country.
That one I fight for....
I got him.
Now he's yours.
I'll be dead,
I'll be coming to earth.'

All these places for us....
all belong Gagadju.
We use them all the time.
Old people used to move around,
camp different place.
Wet season, dry season....
always camp different place.

Wet season....
we camp high place,
get plenty goose egg.
No trouble for fresh water.

Dry season....
move along floodplain,
billabong got plenty food.
Even food there when everything dry out.

All Gagudju used to visit....
used to come here to billabong....
dry season camp.
Plenty file snake, long-neck turtle.
Early dry season....
good lily.
Just about middle dry season....
file snake, long-neck turtle,
lily flowering.

Everybody camp,
like holiday.
Plenty food this place.
Good time for ceremony,
stay maybe one or two weeks.

Pelican, Jabiru, White Cockatoo....
all got to come back,
make him like before.

Fish....
he listen.
He say
'Oh, somebody there.'
Him frightened,
too many Toyota.
Make me worry too.

I look after my country,
now lily coming back.
Lily, nuts, birds, fish....
whole lot coming back.

We got to look after,
can't waste anything.
We always used what we got....
old people and me.

If man leave one or two barramundi behind
he go bad.... trouble....
big fight.
He can't waste anything.

My culture's hard,
but got to be to keep him.
If you waste him anything now,
next year.... you can't get as much,
because you already waste.

When I was young I never wasted,
otherwise straight away I get trouble.
Even bone not wasted,
Make soup or burn that bone.
Watch out....
That might be dreaming one too

That story change him now.
It should still be,
but young people won't listen.
Just chuck him away....
waste him,
destroy everything.

When we young....
my time, Felix's time,
we never eat big fish.
That fish for old people.

Same for goose.
Young people only eat shoulder of goose,
older people must have goose first.
Same for Oenpelli, Mary River, all over.

If young people eat goose or fish,
then he'll be dead.
No young people touch him big fish or goose.
If touch him,
law says got to die.

You know frill-neck lizard?
He look funny.
Used to be good smooth animal.
He was man.
He done something wrong.
Look ugly now....
skinny leg, arm,
big one ear....
frill-neck.
What he done?
Break law.

He went to sacred ceremony....
called Ubarr.
He didn't listen....
clapping hands.
Old people tell him
'You break law,
you'll be skinny,
you won't grow more.
People will see you like that.'

And he went like that....
big ear.
'You'll be like that for ever and ever.'

Lizard say,
'You make me back like I was before.'
People say 'No,
you break law.
You got to stay like that....
it's law.'
We can't break law.
No, we can't break law.
That frill-neck lizard done it first,
now look how thin he is....
that his own fault.
He spoilt ceremony.
We can't change it....
that's law.

Land

People....
they can't listen for us.
They just listen for money....
money.

We want goose, we want fish.
Other men want money.
Him can make million dollars,
but only last one year.
Next year him want another million.
Forever and ever him make million dollars....
him die.

Million no good for us.
We need this earth to live because....
we'll be dead,
we'll become earth.

This ground and this earth....
like brother and mother.

Trees and eagle....
you know eagle?
He can listen.
Eagle our brother,
like dingo our brother.

We like this earth to stay,
because he was staying for ever and ever.

We don't want to lose him.
We say 'Sacred, leave him.'

Goanna is dead because they cutting its body off us,
cutting our mother's belly,
grandpa's bones.
They squash him up....
no good,
and carve up our earth....
no good.

We come from earth....
bones.
We go to earth....
ashes.

My children got to hang onto this story.
This important story.
I hang onto this story all my life.
My father tell me this story.
My children can't lose it.

White European want to know....
asking 'What this story?'
This not easy story.
No-one else can tell it....
because this story for Aboriginal culture.

I speak English for you,
so you can listen....
so you can know....
you will understand.
If I put my words (language) in same place,
you won't understand.

Our story is in the land....
it is written in those sacred places.
My children will look after those places,
that's the law.

No-one can walk close to those sacred places.
No difference for Aborigine or white European,
that's the law.
We can't break law.

Old people tell me,
'You got to keep law.'
'What for?' I said.
'No matter we die but that law....
you got to keep it.
No camping in secret place,
no fire there,
no play for kids.
You can't break law.
Law must stay.'

When that law started?
I don't know how many thousands of years.
European say 40,000 years,
but I reckon myself probably was more because....
it is sacred.

Dreaming place....
you can't change it,
no matter who you are.
No matter you rich man,
no matter you king.
You can't change it.

We say that's secret because dreaming there.
We frightened you might get hurt if you go there....
not only my country but any secret place.
No matter if it Croker Island, Elcho Island, Brisbane or
Sydney.

Wherever, you'll get him same
because that secret place not small.
Secret place is biggest one,
everywhere....
powerful.

We walk on earth,
we look after....
like rainbow sitting on top.
But something underneath,
under the ground....
we don't know....
you don't know.

What you want to do?
If you touch....
you might get cyclone, heavy rain or flood.
Not just here,
you might kill someone in another place.
Might be kill him in another country.
You cannot touch him.

These very important places,
but we frightened that European might touch him.
If we tell white European story,
he slow to listen.
If we get little bit wild,
he might listen....
but slow.

Him got to always ask question.
He want that place.
That's why we frightened.

I worry about that place....
secret place.
That got painting there,
inside cave.
It got to be looked after because
my father, grandad all look after.
Now me,
I got to do same.

If that painting get rubbed off
there might be big trouble.
That important story.
It for all round this area.
That biggest story....
biggest place.

My grandpa teach me.
That painting is true.
Fish, python, goose,
all painting there.
Grandpa say
'You see painting,
Fish.... you got to eat.
Python.... you got to eat.
Mullet.... you got to eat.
Lily, turtle, all same.
They for you.'

That drawing there.... painting,
that's the size fish should be now.
Used to be that size.
I saw them myself.
Used to be that size at Oenpelli.
Need two men to carry one catfish.
That was when I was nearly man....
still young.

Now?....
Little boy can carry catfish.
Should be 50 pounds,
but only 15 pounds.

You can't see big fish anymore,
not at Oenpelli.
People say,
'Plenty fish there.
You see barramundi'
I say
'Yes, pocket fish.'
They say
'What you mean?'
I tell them,
'Pocket fish that barramundi,
little one.
You can put him in your pocket.'

They tell me
'Big catfish....
We got him plenty.'
I say
'Should be ten times size of that.'

We have to keep pressure on young people to learn.
They must learn these things.
I have to stay on to teach my children.
But, young people spread out (go elsewhere, to towns).
It like that everytime we have meetings,
meeting for business (ceremonies).
We make arrangement....
you know.... appointment,
about business, secret.
Young people all in town.

You look now....
nobody with me.
This old man here (Iyanuk, Felix Holmes)
he with me,
but we don't have a dozen behind us....
So, we must stay on....
Look after and teach.

All my uncle gone,
but this story I got him.
They told me....
they taught me....
and I can feel it.

I feel it with my body,
with my blood.
Feeling all these trees,
all this country
When this wind blow you can feel it.
Same for country....
You feel it.
You can look,
but feeling....
that make you.

Feeling make you,
Out there in open space.
He coming through your body.
Look while he blow and feel with your body....
because tree just about your brother or father....
and tree is watching you.

Earth....
like your father or brother or mother,
because you born from earth.
You got to come back to earth.
When you dead....
you'll come back to earth.
Maybe little while yet....
then you'll come to earth.
That's your bone,
your blood.
It's in this earth,
same as for tree.

Tree....
he watching you.
You look at tree,
he listen to you.
He got no finger,
he can't speak.
But that leaf....
he pumping, growing,
growing in the night.
While you sleeping
you dream something.
Tree and grass same thing.
They grow with your body,
with your feeling.

If you feel sore....
headache, sore body,
that mean somebody killing tree or grass.
You feel because your body in that tree or earth.
Nobody can tell you,
you got to feel it yourself.

Tree might be sick....
you feel it.
You might feel it for 2 or 3 years.
You get weak....
little bit, little bit....
because tree going bit by bit....
dying.

Tree not die when you cut it.
He not die tomorrow,
he still green.
Might be 5 or 6 weeks,
might be 2 months.
You feel it then....
your body....
you feel it.

Environment

Those trees....
they grow and grow.
Every night they grow.
That grass....
no matter it burn.
When it drink,
it grow again.
When you cut tree,
it pump life away,
all the same as blood in my arm.

Earth....
same thing.
You brought up with earth, tree, water.

Water is your blood.
Water....
you can't go without water.
No matter no food 2 days, 3 day, 4 day if you got water.
If no water....
little bit weak....
getting hard.
Water important.

That's why we get story.
Old people tell us about that first lightning.
That's before wet season,
we can't look at it.
Later we get lightning and rain from other way.
But, must not look at first lightning....
bend head down....
like first woman who looked.
She was ashamed and bent her head.
We must do the same.

Sky....
cloud....
made for us.
Star....
he'll stay for ever and ever.

When you laying down in the night
look at star.
I was laying down....
I look star....
It make me remember when I was young.
When young I think that star really river....
river and creek.
You call it Southern Cross,
that other star.
We say it spear and crocodile.
So, I just look.
I remember other star....
eagle....
eagle on other side.

I look at star.
I know just about time for wet season,
may be time for dry season.
I know from star.

Well now that star over here,
so look out for wet season.
That star right down in December.
When that wet season come,
that star come back.
I say
'Well, dry season coming.'
Then rain finish him up.

October....
up high.
November....
getting low.
December....
right down.

My grandpa taught me that.
He said,
'Don't forget this.
Tell this story with kids....
so he can listen....
slow.
And then story will come for him....
exactly like this.
This story right, exactly right,
because it dreaming.'

Death

We all lying down on grass in dry season.
Look up at stars.
I tell kids,
'See them stars....
they been there million years....
they always be there.'

I see pink star.
I tell them 'That King Brown Snake.'
I see his eye....
that pink one.
That star he work.
He go pink, white, pink, white.
That King Brown he look at night.

Eagle,star,
we got him story.
What you call him?
Mars that one....
really eagle.
One arm short,
left wing long one.
His wing been burnt.

Three or four kind of eagle here.
Proper one really that black one.
He can kill him black wallaby.
Proper eagle that one.
Other one with white chest....
he can go billabong or salt water.
But, black one proper eagle.

I look at moon.
It tell me story, like stars.
Moon....
moon is man.
He said
'These people will die,
but they'll come back....
like I do.
They'll come back to be earth again.'

Native Cat said 'No,
they will be dead and never come back.'
Everyone jump on him and kill him.
They burn him so he got plenty spots.
Spots from hot coals.

So moon say again
'Man will come back,
like I come back each time.
He'll come back to earth.'

I know I come back to my country.
When I die I come to (become) earth.
I love this country and this earth.

This story for all people.
Everybody should be listening.
Same story for everyone,
just different language.
My meaning might be little bit hard,
so I speak English.
You just listen careful....
slow.

We got to hang on,
not to lose our story.
Don't think about money too much.
You can get million dollar....
but not worth it.
Million dollar....
he just go 'poof'.
Couple of weeks....
you got nothing.

This ground never move.
I'll be buried here.
I'll be with my brother, my mother.
If I lose this,
where I'll be buried?
I'm hanging onto this ground.
I'll become earth again.
I belong to this earth.
And earth should stay with us.

Tree the same as me.
When he get old he'll die.
He'll be dead and burn.
He'll leave his ashes behind.
Tree become earth.

When I die,
I become skeleton.
I'll be in cave.
That way my spirit stay there.
I seen new coffin 3 or 4 times....
no good.
I don't want coffin....
just cave.
Should be keep our law.

Coffin no good for Aborigine,
got to put bones back where they belong.
Man die.
Soon as him ready,
pick him up,
take him.
Take him to cave.
His shadow,
his spirit,
will stay with him.

If you go in cave....
you must call out.
If you've got young man with you,
he might be stranger for that cave,
for that spirit.
You got to call out first.
You must signal,
must sing out because old people used to tell us
'Your father,
your grandad
your aunty
they'll be waiting for you.
Call out,
they'll listen.
They'll know you,
and they say
'That stranger
we can't hurt him'.'

Old people tell me....
'When you dead you'll be buried.
Uncle bury you in sacred place.'
They told me....
'Don't be rough in your life.
If you too rough....
little bit mistake.'
I said
'What mistake?
No-one can kill me with spear.'
They say
'Yes, we know.
Nobody kill you on outside.
No mark in your body,
but inside....
When you feeling sick,
sick in your body.
Headache is nothing.
But in your body,
get very bad sick.'
I ask 'Why?'
They say
'See that big tree?'
I said
'Yes. I chop him down that tree.
I play,
I cut him.'

'You cut yourself' they say.
'When you maybe 40 years, might be 50 years old,
you feel pain in your back.
Because you cut tree.
I'm old man' he said.
'I'm telling you.'

Land got to stay,
always stay same.
No matter little track....
grass still grow,
bush can grow.
But soon as bitumen there,
all finished.
Grass don't grow.
Maybe little bit side,
but middle.... nothing.
You look where timber.
Gone, pulled out.
Bulldozer rip it out.
Well, you feel it in your body.
You say
'That tree same as me.'
This piece of ground he grow you.

Conclusion

Rock stays,
earth stays.
I die and put my bones in cave or earth.
Soon my bones become earth....
all the same.
My spirit has gone back to my country....
my mother.

This story is important.
It won't change,
it is law.
It is like this earth,
it won't move.

Ground and rock....
he can't move.
Cave....
he never move.
No-one can shift that cave,
because it dream.
It story,
it law.

This law,....
this country....
this people....
No matter what people....
red, yellow, black or white....
the blood is the same.
Lingo little bit different....
but no matter.
Country....
you in other place
But same feeling.
Blood....
bone....
all the same.

This story....
this is true story.

My people....
all dead.
We only got few left....
that's all.
Not many.
We getting too old.
Young people....
I don't know if they can hang onto this story.
But, now you know this story,
and you'll be coming to earth.
You'll be part of earth when you die.
You responsible now.
You got to go with us....
to earth.
Might be you can hang on....
hang onto this story....
to this earth.

You got children....
grandson.
Might be your grandson will get this story....
keep going....
hang on like I done.

Neidjie wisdom.

'Our story is in the land ....
it is written in those sacred places.
My children will look after those places,
that's the law.

Dreaming place ....
you can't change it, no matter who you are.
No matter you rich man, no matter you king.
You can't change it.'

Indjuwanydjuwa.

Bill Neidjie at Ubirr.

Should be written way Aborigine was live.
That floodplain....
my father, my mother, my grandfather
all used to hunt there,
use ironwood spear.
No clothes then.

This earth....
I never damage,
I look after.
Fire is nothing,
just clean up.
When you burn,
New grass coming up.
That mean good animal soon....
might be goose, long-neck turtle, goanna, possum.
Burn him off....
new grass coming up,
new life all over.

Broiling turtle.

Rotten tree....
you got to burn him.
Use him to cook.
He's finished up....
cook or roast in coals.
White European cook in oven....
from university that.
Aborigine didn't know that before.
Now all this coming up with Toyota.

Power station.

Aboriginal painting pipes –
Ranger Uranium.

First people come to us,
they started and run our life.... quick.
They bring drink.
First they should ask about fish, cave, dreaming, but....
they rush in.
They make school.... teach.
Now Aborigine losing it,
losing everything.
Nearly all dead my people,
my old people gone.

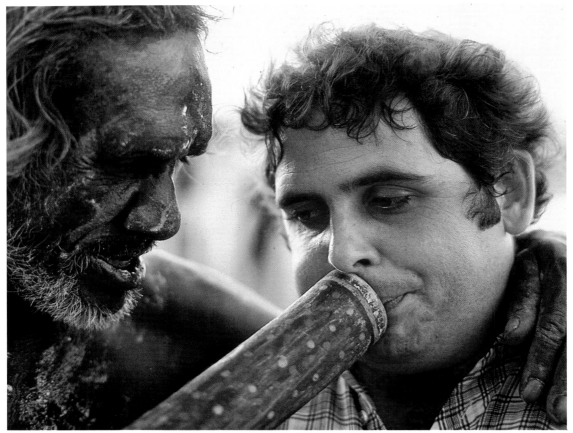

Tuning in.

Skin can be different,
but blood same.
Blood and bone....
all same.
Man can't split himself.

White European can't say
'Oh, that Aborigine no good.'
Might be that Aborigine alright.
Man can't growl at Aborigine,
Aborigine can't growl at white European....
Because both ways.
Might be both good men,
might be both no good....
you never know.

So you should get understand yourself.
No matter Aborigine or white European.

Hunting egret.

Look!

Creek, plain, hill.
That plain can change....
wet season, him mud.
You get lily,
you get fish.
But, he dry up....
that's alright.
Then people can get long-neck turtle
Same for animal.
People look for food,
animal look for food.
Lizard look,
bird look,
anyone look.
We all same.

Long-necked Turtle.

Barramundi.

Rain for us....
for anybody.
Rain give us everything new....
yam, fish, everything.

Wet Season.

We always used what we got . . .
old people and me.
I look after my country,
now lily coming back.
Lily, nuts, birds, fish . . .
whole lot coming back.
We got to look after,
can't waste anything.

Varied Lorikeet.

Waterlilies.

Look after everything.

You know frill-neck lizard?
He look funny.
Used to be good smooth animal.
He was man.
He done something wrong.
Look ugly now....
skinny leg, arm,
big one ear....
frill-neck.
What he done?
Break law.

Frilled Lizard.

People....
they can't listen for us.
They just listen for money....
money.

We want goose, we want fish.
Other men want money.
Him can make million dollars,
but only last one year.
Next year him want another million.
Forever and ever him make million dollars....
him die.

Becoming earth.

Million no good for us.
We need this earth to live because....
we'll be dead,
we'll become earth.

This ground and this earth....
like brother and mother.

Our story is in the land....
it is written in those sacred places.
My children will look after those places,
that's the law.

Dreaming place....
you can't change it,
no matter who you are.
No matter you rich man,
no matter you king.
You can't change it.

My children got to hang onto this story.
This important story.
I hang onto this story all my life.
My father tell me this story.
My children can't lose it.

The dreaming.

When that law started?
I don't know how many thousands of years.
European say 40,000 years,
but I reckon myself probably was more because....
it is sacred.

A Kakadu gallery.

My grandpa teach me.
That painting is true.
Fish, python, goose,
all painting there.
Grandpa say
'You see painting,
Fish.... you got to eat.
Python.... you got to eat.
Mullet.... you got to eat.
Lily, turtle, all same.
They for you.'

That drawing there.... painting,
that's the size fish should be now.
Used to be that size.
I saw them myself.
Used to be that size at Oenpelli.
Need two men to carry one catfish.
That was when I was nearly man....
still young.

Now?....
Little boy can carry catfish.

I feel it with my body,
with my blood.
Feeling all these trees,
all this country
When this wind blow you can feel it.
Same for country....
You feel it.
You can look,
but feeling....
that make you.

While you sleeping
you dream something.
Tree and grass same thing.
They grow with your body,
with your feeling.

Water is your blood.
Water . . .
you can't go without water.

Those trees . . .
they grow and grow.
Every night they grow.

When you cut tree,
it pump life away,
all the same as blood in my arm.

May be time for dry season.
I know from star.

Well now that star over here,
so look out for wet season.
That star right down in December.
When that wet season come.
That star come back.
I say,
'Well, dry season coming.'
Then rain finish him up.

October....
up high.
November....
getting low.
December....
right down.

Height of the dry.

Pre-wet season lightning.

My grandpa taught me that.
He said,
'Don't forget this.
Tell this story with kids....
so he can listen....
slow.
And then story will come for him....
exactly like this.
This story right, exactly right,
because it dreaming.'

Now Aborigine losing it,
losing everything.
Nearly all dead my people,
my old people gone.

Still Aborigine all around 1929....
1952, 1953 few left but....
1970 to 1979.... gone.
Only me, Robin Gaden and Felix

Felix Holmes.

Wet season storm approaching.

85

So moon say again
'Man will come back,
like I come back each time.
He'll come back to earth.'

I look at moon.
It tell me story, like stars.
Moon....
moon is man.
He said
'These people will die,
but they'll come back....
like I do.
They'll come back to be earth again.'

Native Cat said 'No,
they will be dead and never come back.'
Everyone jump on him and kill him.
They burn him so he got plenty spots.
Spots from hot coals.

I know I come back to my country.
When I die I come to (become) earth.
I love this country and this earth.

Back to earth.

Northern Native Cat.

Death.

This story for all people.
Everybody should be listening.
Same story for everyone,
just different language.

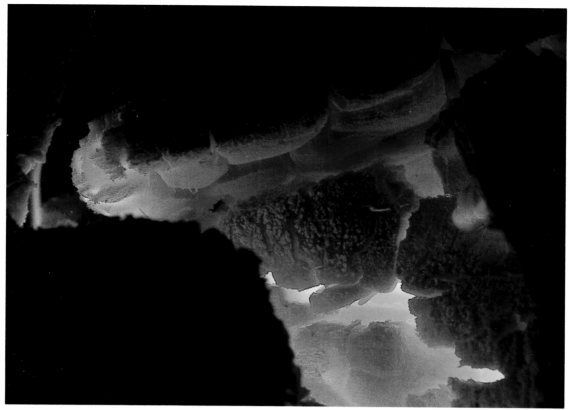

Conversion.

This ground never move.
I'll be buried here.
I'll be with my brother, my mother.
If I lose this,
where I'll be buried?
I'm hanging onto this ground.
I'll become earth again.
I belong to this earth.
And earth should stay with us.

Tree the same as me.
When he get old he'll die.
He'll be dead and burn.
He'll leave his ashes behind.
Tree become earth.

Resurection.

Iridiyu—2,000 generations
of spirits.

Rock stays,
earth stays.
I die and put my bones in cave or earth.
Soon my bones become earth....
all the same.
My spirit has gone back to my country....
my mother.

This story is important.
It won't change,
it is law.
It is like this earth,
it won't move.

This law,....
this country....
this people....
No matter what people....
red, yellow, black or white....
the blood is the same.
Lingo little bit different....
but no matter.
Country....
you in other place
But same feeling.
Blood....
bone....
all the same.

Big Bill and Felix Holmes.

My people....
all dead.
We only got few left....
that's all.
Not many.
We getting too old.
Young people....
I don't know if they can hang onto this story.
But, now you know this story,
and you'll be coming to earth.
You'll be part of earth when you die.
You responsible now.
You got to go with us....
to earth.
Might be you can hang on....
hang onto this story....
to this earth.

You got children....
grandson.
Might be your grandson will get this story....
keep going....
hang on like I done.

The future.

'My spirit has gone back to
my country... my mother'

I belong to this earth
and earth stay with us . . .
forever.

Acknowledgements

Photographs

Photographers are listed in the order their images appear, from left to right from the top of the page.

Cover (Bill Neidjie): Stephen Davis. Back Cover (Corella Tree, East Alligator): Ian Morris. 1: Stephen Davis. 2-3: Ian Morris. 4-5: Ian Morris. 8: Greg Miles. 9: Allan Fox. 10: Ian Morris. 12: Colin Totterdell. 13: Allan Fox. 16: Allan Fox; Ian Morris; Ian Morris. 17: Allan Fox; Greg Miles; Allan Fox. 18: Greg Miles; Allan Fox; Allan Fox. 19: All by Allan Fox. 20: All by Allan Fox. 21: Ian Morris; Peter Jarver; Peter Jarver. 22: Allan Fox. 23: Ian Morris. 26: Stephen Davis. 27: Jack Stokes Collection, Australian Archives. 28: Ian Morris. 29: Stephen Davis. 30: Stephen Davis. 31: Stephen Davis. 32: Stephen Davis. 65: Allan Fox. 66: Allan Fox. 67: Ian Morris; Allan Fox. 68: Stephen Davis; Allan Fox. 69: Peter Jarver. 70: Steve Parish. 71: Allan Fox. 72: Peter Jarver. 73: All by Allan Fox. 74: All by Ian Morris. 75: Stephen Davis. 76: Stephen Davis. 77: Ian Morris. 78: Allan Fox; Ian Morris; Ian Morris. 79: Stephen Davis. 80-81: Allan Fox. 82: Allan Fox; Ian Morris. 83: Ian Morris. 84: Allan Fox; Ian Morris. 85: Stephen Davis; Ian Morris. 86: Chris Harris. 87: Stephen Davis; Ian Morris. 88: Allan Fox. 89: Allan Fox. 90: Allan Fox. 91: Stephen Davis. 92: Stephen Davis. 93: Stephen Davis. 94-95: Allan Fox. 96: NASA.

Original Artwork:
Jane Moore

Printing:
Prestige Litho, Brisbane, Queensland, Australia.

Igalka.

Swamp hunting
ground
turtle, barramundi
file snake,
wild honey,
lily,
geese

Camp of
Dolly Yann

Nabädi
High ground –
Spring with fresh
water

W
Sh
Bi
ste
as
ch

Nawarrkpil
Big Cave
for camping
in wet

Lots of Yams

Mamul
Dry Season
Camp

Jane Moore.